Invisible

Poems and Aphorisms

Timothy Donohue

Copyright © 2016 by Timothy Donohue
All rights reserved.
ISBN-13: 978-1-950186-10-5

Cover photograph by Timothy Donohue
Cover design and interior layout by Jennifer Leigh Selig

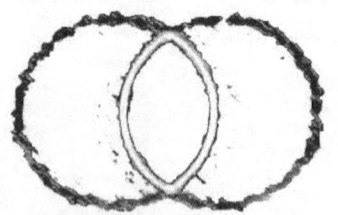

MANDORLA BOOKS
CARPINTERIA, CA
WWW.MANDORLABOOKS.COM

For Mara, who saw invisibilities, and stayed.

CONTENTS

Publisher's Foreword by Jennifer Leigh Selig   i
Poems and Aphorisms by Timothy Donohue   1

Invisible	3
What It's About	5
Lives In A Coma	7
A Few Lucky Things	9
ADU	11
Rainfall	15
Old Gets	17
Only The Silence	21
The Doctor Will Explain Everything	23
Memory Of My Daughter Talking To Her Doll About Life and Poetry	27
Definitions Of Rest	29
The Loss Of Loss	31
Photographic Memory	33
The Silence Poem	37
Shared Custody	39
The Novel's Last Call	41

The Snow Trees In The Yard Of The Failed Suicide	47
Winter Weekend	49
Yes, Cancer	51
A Kind Of Space	53
Because You Asked	57
We Wish You A Happy Birthday	59
Aphorisms	61
K Sends Me Her Poems	83
The Preferred Embrace	85
Notes From The Last Time I Saw Ferlinghetti	87
The Poems You Will Never Read	93
At A Graveyard By An Orchard	95
Application Denied	97
Why I Don't Ask You To Pray (The Big Sunlight)	99
What The Words Remember	101
Excerpt From "The Book Of Revelations" (a longer work)	103
The British Emergency Warning System	105
Letter Of Response	107
We Are Appetite To The Stars	113
Visiting The Novelist	115
Pease Porridge Cold	117
The Thing Itself	119
Bones And Breath	121

Choices	123
February 18th, Twenty-seven Miles Away	125
Handshakes And Mirrors	127
In An Unmappable Place	131
Finding The Median	133
You	135
Death Comes In The Kitchen	137
Like A Vapor In The Head	139
"Invisible" (Draft Image)	141
Afterword by Laura Kennelly	145
About the Author	147
Acknowledgments	149

PUBLISHER'S FOREWORD

BY JENNIFER LEIGH SELIG

"No publisher should ever express an opinion on the value of what he publishes. That is a matter entirely for the literary critic to decide. I can quite understand how any ordinary critic would be strongly prejudiced against a work that was accompanied by a premature and unnecessary panegyric from the publisher. A publisher is simply a useful middle-man. It is not for him to anticipate the verdict of criticism."

~Oscar Wilde

In 2015, I became a useful "middle-man" (though I prefer the term "midwife"), publishing a collection of selected poems by three talented poets—Dennis Patrick Slattery, Donald Carlson and Timothy Donohue—titled *Road, Frame, Window: A Poetics of Seeing*. It was my first introduction to the poetry of Timothy Donohue, and I was an immediate and unabashed fan.

And I wanted more.

After the book was in print, I sent Tim a message asking if he had more poems lying in wait, and if so, could I publish them. Though it is true that I was reaching out to him as a publisher, it is in fact truer that I was reaching out to him as a reader. The great American writer Toni Morrison once said, "If there's a book that you want to read, but it hasn't been written yet, then you must write it." The same goes for publishing: if there's a book that you want to read, but it hasn't been published yet, then you must publish it.

And so I did.

Rather than offering "a premature and unnecessary panegyric from the publisher" and offending the delightful Oscar Wilde, I will leave it to the literary critics to offer "the verdict of criticism." They can comment on Mr. Donohue's stanza structure, his choice of caesura, his enjoyment of enjambment, whether his quatrains and refrains entertain, and whether he left the meter running for an appropriate period of time. They can parse his poetry all they want. They can think long and hard about it and then stand up and shout out their learned opinions.

As for me, you'll just find me curled up with a good book.

How do I know it's a good book? I know as a reader, not as a publisher. I know in the same way Emily Dickinson knew powerful poetry: "If I feel physically as if the top of my head were taken off, I know *that* is poetry." She asked, "Is there any other way?"

Yes, Emily, there are other ways. If you feel physically as if your heart needs new chambers to contain the flow of emotions, you know *that* is poetry. If you feel physically as if your stomach has sinking feelings and it will take some time until you're buoyant again, you know *that* is poetry. If you feel physically as if your eyes are quick to tear up or your throat to issue a hearty ha-ha, you know *that* is poetry. Capable critics may know with their minds, but sensitive readers know with their bodies, and this I know—this book you are holding in your hands, *this* is poetry.

September 5, 2016
Jennifer Leigh Selig, Mandorla Books
www.mandorlabooks.com

INVISIBLE

Poems and Aphorisms

Only the hand that erases can write the true thing.
~Meister Eckhart

Invisible

1.
I stood in line behind a fragrance.
It was you. Your face was invisible,
But it was you.
This was a long time ago.

2.
An electric door kept opening and closing.
Pushing your scent deep inside me,
And urging me to say something clever
To the back of your head.

3.
Inside everyone is a door
They will not open,
And a door they will not close—
Choices must be made.

4.
I should have made you laugh.
Said some nonsense about
Your oolong tea or the candy bar
With the same name as your father

But I remained invisible.

~Invisible Candy~

What It's About

I hand you a poem
You say, "what's it about?"

This is what it's about

"I know" you say
But how did you get this?
"You mean the poem?"

"Yes, of course I mean the poem"
That's what I'm asking
Oh, I don't know that

But this is about you
About you asking
What the poem is "about"

About is always
Exactly the same thing
"What's that?"

The thing you haven't read yet

~Invisible Candy~

~Invisible Hand~

Lives In A Coma

1.
Sometimes I wonder
If there was another way,
An ending we might have missed…
It was late morning
It was the end of summer
Cars came infrequently past that motel
A dog barked
Then silence would return,
Coating our lips
And closing our eyes

2.
We played hooky from real love for so long
We lied about our whereabouts so often
Sometimes we forgot our real names…
Everything outside that room was always boiled
Inside we pulled black curtains
Against the heat and falling bombs
Of sunlight and friends…

3.
No. There was no other way, no other ending…
It was late morning
It was the end of summer
We hugged so hard
We put our lives in a coma—
And left, in separate cars

~Invisible Hand~

~Invisible Curtains~   ~Invisible Candy~

A Few Lucky Things

The way frost
Leaves a note
On a window in winter

The size of the moon
On a day you lost
More than you should

A missed phone call
A line in a poem

~Invisible Curtains~

~Invisible Note~   ~Invisible Hand~

~Invisible Candy~

ADU

1.
All cars must squeeze into one lane
Directly before the entrance to the bridge,
Usually a slow huddle, without touching or talking

Brake, coast, roll and cross over…
It's a safe play for a long time,
Doesn't mean much when you're 20, 30 or 40

A few years later, a truth cracks wide open inside you:

We're going straight from here to the absence of
    everything
We're dropping down from this suddenly unfinished
    bridge
Pumping the brake pedal like crazy

2.
The beautiful, the groomed to succeed,
Often miss this cracked-open sense of doom
To them, death is more like an unbreakable bad habit, a
    nuisance

And when it comes, they know it will be
Dutifully swift, a blown artery, or an inoperable mass
Under the numb of drugs, with time to put things in
    order…

A seasoned blond in a half-top black Mercedes cuts in
Exposing a license plate that reads "ADU"
Excited, I yell out to her, Yes! That's Right! You're right!

~Invisible Brake~

But there's no place or time to turn around
And the hole in the bridge is straight ahead
She looks in her rearview mirror, and mouths:

Goodbye

~Invisible Brake~

~Invisible Hole~

Rainfall

1.
Rain doesn't believe in mist or fog
Or countless shades of grey
Rain doesn't care about "meaning"
Or how well something is said
Especially something called "poetry"

2.
A fall
Is a fall
Is a fall
Says rain…

3.
Rain is a see-through thing
That pushes your real voice
Below your mouth
Dragging your words
Down to earth
Where they pool and puddle
And wait for a long stare of sunlight

To return them to air

~Invisible Hole~

~Invisible Puddle~   ~Invisible Brake~

Old Gets

1.
Old gets to the conscience first
The client, the class, the whatever
It is you can't believe

2.
Nothing to do with
Three-hundred-and-sixty degrees
Or three-hundred-sixty-five days
Times (x)

3.
A woman fills your head
Like a flower print dress
A first and forever-lost love
The one who kissed and said
"Listen. Listen
To the saxophone
Stars"

4.
The steering wheel
Suddenly appears
You wake up driving
You know you're coming
You know you're going
Nothing in between

5.
A question fills your head
Like a broken bottle of perfume
"Who? Who is the librarian
Of Hearts?"

~Invisible Puddle~

~Invisible Client~   ~Invisible Hole~

~Invisible Brake~

6.
You pass a truck
Trail another
A car comes alongside
You wave. She passes,
Looking at you in her mirror
Her eyes, dark and angry

7.
You're in the driveway
The lawn. The house.
It all looks new at night
You stop at the door
You step back, you lean
Your ear to the sky

8.
You can get old playing make-believe
But comes a lover you wouldn't believe
And you'll be ancient
For the rest of your days
Forgetting yourself in public
And never, never forgiving

~Invisible House~

Only The Silence

I repeat your name
And nothing changes
We reappear to disappear

Words that should never have been said
And the moment where I could have disagreed
Come and go just the same…

But in the forever presence
And forever absence
Of this summoning

We always appear
To be younger and younger
It's just the silence

Only the silence
That seems to age

~Invisible House~

~Invisible Presence~

The Doctor Will Explain Everything

After the colonoscopy
Surgery was scheduled
"Though I can't imagine
When that would be"
We nodded as if we understood

What a shame you said
Only two days ago
After sunset
We strolled through the garden
Put flowers by the birdbath,
And dad spoke softly

(Mom kept his schedule open, in case of emergencies)

To calm her fears,
She went online
For more information
And took some time
For a much needed vacation

Then with much consideration
He made his decision
He decided to join a gym
To get in shape
He bought more broth

We gathered in a blue-green room
With yellowed brown chairs
Years ago, expectant fathers
Would wait there, wait and
Smoke, wait and smoke

A groggy surgeon said she would begin

~Invisible Presence~

~Invisible Birdbath~   ~Invisible House~

As soon as we put on
Plenty of sunscreen
(Whenever I remember,
I smile)

There were instructions:
Whether you like it or not,
You have to go to bed now…
Take this medication for pain
As often as needed

There were revelations:
No matter how many times I try to stop,
I can't give up chocolate…
Sometimes I don't clean
Under the bed

She slammed the door in a huff
We nodded as if we understood

~Invisible Birdbath~

~Invisible Bed~   ~Invisible Presence~

~Invisible House~

**Memory Of My Daughter Talking
To Her Doll About Life And Poetry**

Mommy says she needs sleep
Daddy says he needs shock treatment

I think he's going to stick his finger
In that thing in the wall

You need a bath brown baby
But I won't make you wash your hair

Daddy writes poetry
I can write my name and seven words

Timothy Barbara Cat (and)
I Love You (and) Sarah

Something is called dictation
Where you say a poem without a pen

I told mommy this poem

The squirrel ran up the tree
And a poem fell down on me

I have to practice violin now

~Invisible Squirrel~

Definitions Of Rest

What you hope
Will turn to sleep

A sporting lie
About the bench

What the arm seeks
In airplanes

A calling to
In obituaries

What the weary
Will never get

A symbol of silence
In music

The word the jury
Is waiting for

The opposite
Of bodies in motion

The length of your life
At the beginning of love

~Invisible Squirrel~

~Invisible Jury~

The Loss Of Loss

Before they're not terrible
So many things are terrible
Before you realize

They were never terrible
Before you see
Just how unterrible
Things really can be

Such loss of anticipated loss is hard to reconcile...

What will give us meaning
What will be our pleasure
What will make us feel whole

When there is no broken thing
No grief to fill with accusations
No anguish to walk alongside us
With angry theories

About the nature of happiness

~Invisible Jury~

~Invisible Happiness~   ~Invisible Squirrel~

Photographic Memory

Most is unremembered

Names gone
clean off
faces

Erased
by days
dragging

Sunlit skies
over an unstable
photo finish

Hometowns
imminent weddings
all deleted—

Gone
the years this album
laid open

To this page
unprotected
from the moons

That pulled
"the Movement"
and all our politics

Out of the picture

What remains
is the unnatural strength
of leftover love

~Invisible Happiness~

~Invisible Weddings~   ~Invisible Jury~

~Invisible Squirrel~

A focus
zoomed
to the important familiar—

Two plastic cups
filled to the brim
with gin

The fact
that only I
knew

The only thing
you wore under
that red dress

Was perfume

~Invisible Dress~

The Silence Poem

The white sheet of paper
Before the poem

Your lips reading
These words to yourself

All the snow that fell
Past the windows
Of my childhood home

Me somewhere else
Thinking these thoughts

~Invisible Dress~

~Invisible Lips~

Shared Custody

Up late
Stand-up
Dinner
Sliced onion
Celery

Open can
Of salmon

...

Up too
(In his down
Below)
The cat
With shared
Custody

Of all hunger
And darkness

~Invisible Lips~

~Invisible Onion~ ~Invisible Dress~

The Novel's Last Call

Part One

I was in the shower.
The message she left
Was borderline threatening:
"We have to meet. Things have changed.
You're avoiding me. I won't have it!
Call me as soon as you get this!"
A cup of coffee
Crept to the left in my stomach.
Suddenly, my towel seemed inadequate.
"Oh! Not this again!" I thought.
"Proza otstoy"* I said out loud.

You deserve a little background…

Many years ago, we had a torrid affair.
Like most affairs, it was unplanned.
As a gray Moscow sky spun frost on windows,
Candlelight reflected her ink-dark eyes in a samovar.
We both put excessive amounts of sugar and lemon in our
    tea,
Which reminded us that we had met before,
At a huge rented dacha near St. Petersburg
Owned by our mutual friend Arkady Karamazov.
And with those tea cup admissions and further recognitions,
Our lust for each other began.

Part Two

And then, and then and then…
There was the mugging near the pawnshop in the bad part of
    Leningrad

~Invisible Onion~

~Invisible Samovar~   ~Invisible Lips~

~Invisible Dress~

There was Ariel, the dark mistress whose red lips were
    actually tattoos
There was the warm, womblike ground that brought us
    potatoes
The summer we fled Leningrad for Petrograd.

Can I tell you something?

When you love a woman like that
Your heart becomes a semicolon.
You are all "and"
You are all "but"
You are all "for"
But most of all,

You are forbidden to be alone.

Part Three

I cannot love you anymore.
You have too much to say, and too much to do.
Parts of Cleveland no longer look like Moscow,
But still, I am happy here.
Besides there are other things for you to dislike—
I am gray now, and wear glasses.
My ability to drink one-handed
From the silver samovar is gone.

I can no longer mistake vodka
For water, on purpose.
And like my poems,
I get shorter and shorter
With each passing year.
But most of all, I can no longer shrink
From your stature
And your armies of readers
Waiting to be born.

~Invisible Potatoes~

Part Four

I am not changing my number.
I am not moving back to Moscow.
I no longer love
To hear you speak.
I remember your beauty—and I agree:
You deserve to know more
Than the few readers of this poem…
But "goodbye" is now the longest thing,
The only thing,
I can say.

* "prose is shit"

~Invisible Potatoes~

~Invisible Readers~

The Snow Trees In The Yard Of The Failed Suicide

(Crataegus laevigta)

Near the house there's a river
A place to land a small plane, a boat dock
And 9,910 square miles of water

It was May, but bitter winds returned
Shoveling lumps of refrozen river and slushy waves
Against the receding shoreline

A large yard slopes to the lake
Where a new dog barks in a blizzard of Hawthorn petals
Joy and wonder at such sweet tasting snow

A figure at a window
A recitation of failures
A decision to slip under 9,910 square miles of water

But the Hawthorn tree can make it snow in May—

Stopping the sorrowful in their footsteps
And filling the gaps in broken hearts
With a forgotten otherness

~Invisible Readers~

~Invisible Petals~   ~Invisible Potatoes~

Winter Weekend

Small winter light
Climbs the sheets
To our eyelids

Fog floats
Above night-let
Snow

We float too

Drifting back
To where
We were

Minutes or years ago

And closing
The cracks
Behind us…

It's Saturday

Maybe Sunday

~Invisible Petals~

~Invisible Eyelids~   ~Invisible Readers~

~Invisible Potatoes~

Yes, Cancer

Life is all "Yes"
And all else
Is Lack of "Yes"

Cancer is a "Yes"
We don't like so much
But there it is—alive

Nodding, waving
Settling in, getting comfortable
And killing you

Which kills itself…

Which makes cancer
The very last "Yes"
Either of you can be

~Invisible Waving~

A Kind Of Space

I thought
I could
Forget you

Create
A kind
Of space

That would stretch
Until it broke free
Completely

Rope-ends
Of goodbye
Snapping

And falling
Quietly down
The gap

Between us

I thought
We could live
In a space

Between parallel lives

The kind
Of distance
Where the familiar

Is easily
Mistaken
For something else

~Invisible Waving~

~Invisible Stretch~

Like the horizon
Of a field
Or a sunset

At sea

Where a farmer
Tills until
He's one

With the tree line

And a sail
Becomes
A cloud

...

I thought
I could create
A space

Where people
Are seen
Then seem

To disappear
Into someone else

~Invisible Stretch~

~Invisible Cloud~   ~Invisible Waving~

Because You Asked

1.
If I told you
What you mean to me
You would ask "why?" again
And I would lie again
Because I can't say

2.
I've lost
Who you are
Like keys to a car
That drives me near
What I want to hear
But never stops
To let me out

3.
If I told you
What you mean to me
There would be
No safe distance
Between us—
No time to brace
For the crash

~Invisible Horizon~

~Invisible Crash~   ~Invisible Stretch~

~Invisible Waving~

We Wish You A Happy Birthday

We expect you to arrive in a few minutes
We have come to get you out of there
We are sorry for your loss

We hope you like it here
We hope you don't laugh at what we've done with the place
We came a long time ago

We tried to do the right things
We think you can do better

We wish you a happy birthday

We are sorry for your loss

APHORISMS

Kindness isn't exceptional. It's a necessity. Without acts of shared self-concern, isolation shouts down who we really are.

~

He hit the ball so hard it landed in another sport.

~

Beware the cudgel that is honesty that hasn't been proofread.

~

Choosing to write a poem that always employs the template of a rhyme scheme isn't a failure or even a shortcut. But it is like being afraid to go out at night without a flashlight.

~

Is it just bad? Or is it bad enough to be awesome? The hardliners would say intention is everything and the unintentional isn't art at all. I don't buy that. High calorie, low nourishment mind-fat is often tasty.

~

I forget more and more things. But absence reminds me of a previous, perfect pre-everything.

~

Blood rushes to the fists and words to the tongue. The body transfuses in anger.

~

Actions may speak louder than words, but they still need an editor.

~Invisible Cudgel~

At the concert, someone stole my sneeze.

~

Just put a gusset in your crazy pants and move on.

~

When the hometown team is victorious, we say "we" won. When defeated, we say "they" lost.

~

He ran so far he ran out of ZIP codes.

~

Try to chew and swallow your impatience before you speak.

~

I was there when nothing happened. You were too.

~

Graffiti is an unpleasant way of saying "I was here." So is flatulence.

~

The next time you think the sky is falling, call me. I'll bring my jack.

~

Death is an appointment that we go out of our way to be late for.

~

I sense panic in plump sentences.

~Invisible Cudgel~

~Invisible Gusset~

The self-destructions I have survived help to keep my tongue in proportion when things go well.

~

Failures carve the ego into smaller pieces that are easier for others to swallow. Less risk of choking.

~

We did our best waiting ever, but the waiter still won.

~

Maybe the glass is half-full but all dirty. Then what?

~

Some people seize an opportunity, and then quickly convulse.

~

The difference between pants and trousers was so small, it was put in the dictionary with tweezers.

~

I can't remember what I want to and I can't forget what I need to.

~

Treat others to promises kept.

~

Accessibility does not always mean understandability. Accessibility can be a trick the poem plays, first on the poet, then on the reader of the poem.

~Invisible Gusset~

~Invisible Trousers~   ~Invisible Cudgel~

After the distinction without a difference, comes the clarification without a conclusion.

~

I find it hard to describe the elation I feel when the poem I'm working on finally dismisses me from class, so it can go about the business of being itself in the bigger world.

~

Twenty-four-hour cable news channels abhor a vacuum even more than nature does.

~

Man and dinosaur both dreamed they would some day fly. Both were right.

~

Work the work. Not the tool.

~

I'm grateful for clothes. Without them, nakedness would just mean nothing.

~

Avoid food samples whenever possible. Out of mouth, out of mind, out of waistline.

~

There is no digging a foxhole in the sky.

~

Summer. Sunshine is assumed.

~Invisible Trousers~

~Invisible Dinosaur~   ~Invisible Gusset~

~Invisible Cudgel~

Death means you joined the majority. The number of dead outnumbers the living. There's an odd sort of comfort in that.

~

There are things the heart wants that the head cannot undo.

~

Love isn't divided by gender. But it's subtracted by fear and multiplied by kindness.

~

It is a different kind of house that is built in idleness.

~

At the coffee shop a pair of black shoes, a pair of red shoes. Two women sit whispering, estrogen to estrogen.

~

Saying you read all of James Joyce is not unlike saying you read the Rosetta Stone just before last call.

~

Chances are, long before the coroner actually pronounces you dead, someone in charge of marketing demographics will have already reached that conclusion.

~

Being alive isn't arbitrary. Having a life is.

~

Sadness. The cold light of a dead star.

~Invisible Dead~

Every novel by a poet is a failure to give up writing.

~

Forged in fire, the spoon spends its long grey life amazed that lips never melt on contact.

~

I appreciate and enjoy irony. But I expect sincerity.

~

There was a time when the Beach Boys would sing and sunshine would come out of their mouths.

~

We talk of our past like an ocean. But our present is the ocean; and some "remember when" is just a rain drop by comparison.

~

The strange addition and subtraction we call "aftermath." Numbers for loss. Numbers for found. The square root of grief.

~

In the city, you ingest place. In the country, space. Neither is calorie-free.

~

Elizabethan hookup talk: "to meet, perhaps to swive?"

~

Anger is a gnawing hunger that can make a sandwich out of your life. You disappear, one bite at a time.

~Invisible Dead~

~Invisible Fire~

It's nighttime in the mirror. Who knows who's really there?

~

The violinist tackled a piece by Bartok, but the piece broke free and scored.

~

Western failure: "All hat, no cattle." Eastern failure: "All title, no mettle."

~

Sometimes my thoughts wander around without their glasses on.

~

What is hope? Faith, without belief.

~

Only in art can you use a term like "authentic" copy, without laughing.

~

Failure in an academic setting is a strike against you. Failure in art or invention is good information.

~

Same trash, different curb.

~

What the wind blows in, the rain will wash away and the sun will lose track of.

~Invisible Fire~

~Invisible Violinist~   ~Invisible Dead~

We all have acquaintances that are rarely right in their facts, but never afflicted with doubt.

~

Most like to drive at summer weather speeds: highs in the 80's, lows in the 60's.

~

Some think outside the box and are never heard from again. Some return, on medications.

~

Three people sat on a log. One said he believed in God, one said he didn't, and one said he didn't know one way or another. After the discussion, how many were left on the log?

~

I say things to myself sometimes just to shut me up.

~

Clouds appear. They have their own reasons.

~

The illusion of rage is that, for a moment, you feel as if you are mightily whole; complete, huge, gigantic. In fact, what's happening is a kind of temporary invisibility—you are not yourself, not there—and that is a very, very dangerous place to not be.

~

We live life as an assumption prior to experience. It's the only thing we can do.

~Invisible Violinist~

~Invisible Log~ ~Invisible Fire~

~Invisible Dead~

If the deadest nail is always in a door, where's the liveliest?

~

We can argue about the nature of love. We can even doubt its existence. But not kindness. Kindness is witnessed and understood everywhere. No words required. No translation.

~

Being physically fit requires consistent attempts at improvement during workouts. That means pressing beyond your habitual measures of performance and accepting new levels of discomfort. The same goes for learning. And it never gets easier. In the one case, you get faster and stronger. In the other, more thoughtful and less cocksure ignorant.

~

Some couples are invisible to each other in plain sight; others, like bombs in boxes hidden in the basement.

~

The book fell apart in the hands of my eyes.

~

Susan Sontag famously (and helpfully) stated that "photography recycles the real." But it's an aesthetic observation that shouldn't be limited to photography. Such recycling, or repurposing, or recontexting of artistic exposures is evident in painting, music, poetry and a slew of other things in our cultural atmosphere. It follows that *"quoting"* (in and out of context) is a more accurate description of the creative act and the results thereof. Photography is just one tool in the creative tool bag one brings to a larger creative process. A process that might best be termed *quotography*. The explosion of technology hasn't

~Invisible Boxes~

refuted Ecclesiastes. It made it more prescient.

~

The quotography we find in advertising and other popular aesthetic presences is often a metacliché. The quotography we find in other areas is often a metaphor. Both are quoting two worlds at once. Both affect us with a renewed sense of recognition and wonder.

~

Cast in bronze on manhole covers, "Sanitary Sewer" may be the most visible and durable oxymoron in America.

~

Eat more music. Drink more words.

~

Gravity makes a hole we crawl through until we hit the earth with a thud. Luckily, levity can blow us right back up.

~

I wonder sometimes about "wonder." What constant incompleteness, what state of unfinishedness is permanently alive in all of us. Things without which, wonder cannot be.

~

Time flies. Window seat or aisle? Your choice.

~Invisible Boxes~

~Invisible Window~

K Sends Me Her Poems

K sends me her poems to love
It is all we have left
Of a another kind of love
My lawyer friends
Say it's a dangerous activity
A kind of disorderly conduct
By persisting…
But sometimes
When the distractions
Of the day have signed off
And the night has lost its signal
I have read things
That make me feel
Like we had children
She never told me about
That we loved each other
In ways we wouldn't say
With eyes we wouldn't open…
K sends me her poems
To have and to hold

Like a flashlight

~Invisible Window~

~Invisible Flashlight~   ~Invisible Boxes~

The Preferred Embrace

On a sidewalk,
Snow falls between
A man and a woman
Struggling against late December winds—it's obvious
Their separateness is pre-planned
The snowy gap is precise
And irrevocable.

There is no touching now in these lives.
No looking back, nor at each other.
Just a wobbly march forward,
Into more and more invisibility.

What was the word that sawed them in half?
What failures of desire
Would make falling down,
Alone, under a winter sky,

The preferred embrace.

~Invisible Flashlight~

~Invisible Word~   ~Invisible Window~

~Invisible Boxes~

Notes From The Last Time I Saw Ferlinghetti

> "...there's no there, there."
> Gertrude Stein, *Everybody's Autobiography*

Weekend-ending. Runway-runaway
Dallas to San Francisco 1:10 a.m.
And where I'm heading it's 1986,
But it's still yesterday
So much for the times of our life

I have made a mess of my life
Mixed the mess and painted with it
To outline voices in frames of silence
To take the waiting-for, out of wonder
To hear silence, with new ears

Like a poem, and making
That kind of sense, you left
Ferlinghetti in your Texas college town
And headed to his. You see his motel
Room stuttering, repeating itself in his sleep

Forty-five degrees south by southwest
The machine turned, pointing
A wing at Dallas another
At San Francisco. You hear someone
On the ground pointing a finger
At you. Feathers will fly

The flight attendant leans over
Picking up a napkin. You use the word
"Callipygian" for the first time out loud
She smiles, looking backwards
She is happily confused. She will be
Your friend in the sky
Baudelaire said he wrote to

~Invisible Frames~

"Find the why of it; to transform pleasure
Into knowledge." I do it differently
There is so much
I don't want to know

Between friendship and love
Comes conversational botany
A kind of plant-talk develops
Between a man and a woman
"Nice day." "Yes. I was tired of the rain"

"I see that bridge we were on"
Says a boy to his dad in the seat ahead
When you turn, it's not there anymore
Your lips taste like a woman's cheekbone
Communication from the neck up

"By definition, the poet must be
An enemy of the State" said Ferlinghetti
Afterward, you drove him to where
He would sleep, perhaps to dream
Against the state of Ramada Inn

Tired and unmemorized
You are up to 30,000 feet
And 36 straight hours
You're slipping deeper
Into ball turret 36B

A fish turns in your stomach
It hears the desert below you
It hears the cacti and it hears
The coyotes below you.

There's a "there" there
It's just that whatever is unclear
Must be so cleared away, it takes the waiting-

~Invisible Frames~

~Invisible Botany~

For out of wonder. Like hearing silence
With new ears. Or seeing Ferlinghetti
Ten hours before arriving where he wasn't

Thirty years ago

~Invisible Botany~

~Invisible Ears~   ~Invisible Frames~

The Poems You Will Never Read

1.
The first poem you will never read
Will be in a magazine
You rarely buy
Because the covers do not satisfy

2.
The second poem you will never read
Will be even better than the first one—
And all you had to do was glance at that book
Left open on the airline seat next to you

3.
And so it goes…
Poetic absences and invisibilities surround you, year after year
But how could you know? You with your avoidance issues
And your deep love of *real life*

4.
Finally, according to our records,
The fourth, fifteenth and twenty-seventh poems you will
    never read
Were not your fault. You bought the magazines
But the poems that should have been there

Were forced to disappear by others

~Invisible Ears~

~Invisible Magazines~   ~Invisible Botany~

~Invisible Frames~

At A Graveyard By An Orchard

We know how
The slight rounding
Of a high corner
Means the headstone
Has memorized the wind

We can raise a yellow-gold apple at dusk
And trace with a cool finger
Where the sunlight sat for hours

We are much more invisible than that
We are a name halved backwards
A thousand times

Living changes lives
Until who we are
And who we were
Are less known
Than what the wind
And sunlight did
The day these bodies
Were covered with earth

We are all energy and invisibility
We are all someone
We can only imagine

~Invisible Sunlight~

Application Denied

Your application for Sainthood has been denied
There were numerous gaps
In your *History of Listening* section
And your *Essay on Intercessions* was wanting
More disturbing was the complete lack of any metrics
For evaluating your effectiveness in wish-granting
We will keep your application on file for one year
And we encourage you to keep up the good work
In July we will begin accepting applications for Idols
This position may be of some interest to you

~Invisible Sunlight~

~Invisible Metrics~

Why I Don't Ask You To Pray (The Big Sunlight)

Because you sent me a rosary once
With sharp, shard-like beads
And a ten-page book of instructions
Another time you lit candles
At three different churches
Pumping coins in boxes
Like slot machines made of
Older, better metal

Do you really believe you can whisper
The world into shape?

I know something about miracles
Unexplained recoveries, near annihilations avoided
Justice and kindness erupting from hearts
In the most unlikely places on earth

Things don't change like that because of prayers like that
No matter what they promise you
On Facebook

No

In the Big Sunlight
Things change when you hear
The love of others constantly whispering
That one word inside of you—

Even with your fears
Even as you read this
Even with the darkness
That's bound to fall

On all of us

~Invisible Metrics~

~Invisible Love~   ~Invisible Sunlight~

What The Words Remember

If you look
You will see a book
Laying in sunlight on a table
If you pick it up
You will feel how
It is warm to the center
Where, if you listen
You will hear the words
Remembering what it was like
Somewhere else, in sometime other,
You will hear the hum of stories
About first being called together
By one who knew them all
By their family names
Who argued with them
But loved them all—
One long gone now
Like the strangers
That came later

With names they can never remember

~Invisible Love~

~Invisible Strangers~　　　　　　~Invisible Metrics~

~Invisible Sunlight~

Excerpt from "The Book of Revelations" (a longer work)

XII

> *"Life is lived forwards and understood backwards."*
> ~Soren Kierkegaard

A jagged line of trees breaks cooperatively at the
window of the den. From the birdfeeder in the foreground,
the picture deepens and lengthens; the grass and the
farmer's field deep with snow, and the morning sky
lit like soft soiled bolts of Irish linen: more on the way.
Colored statues come to life. Unposed jays and native
cardinals peck at opposite sides of the provided breakfast:
"When I put something out of my mind,
I subtract a lot of details," says mother
trying to answer one of my questions. And I think
how our lives are most real when we focus on the details
we have given it.

They are the tiny texts of our comings and goings,
Books of Revelation, revealing what we did
with our few years here…But concealing
from us forever, what others will read
into our lives.

~Invisible Details~

The British Emergency Warning System

This as a test
Of The British Emergency Warning System.
This is only a test.

If this were a real emergency
You would be advised
To take this message

Fold it
Into a jaunty hat
And wear it

Until further notice

~Invisible Details~

~Invisible Hat~

Letter Of Response

In response to your request
"What do you think I should do?"
I've gathered together the following:

Rewrite! But read what you have written
Hanging from a chandelier. If one is
Not available, tie a rope between

The refrigerator and the garage door.
Wear only sweat pants! Before you go
To sleep, invent a secret alphabet

In this manner you can marry, divorce,
Sell vinyl siding, survive a serious
Operation and get tenured by age 25!

Yes! Experience is important!
But so much experience is related to fashion!
Spend a day dressed as a postal worker,

A pastry chef, a bus driver and the mascot
Of a football team at a large university.
Resist the easy image! For example

"In every piece of coal, there is a dairy cow."
Such facile familiarity breeds contempt!
Personal relationships are important.

Go to the bus terminal (preferably
One in a city large enough to have
Streets that smell like hamburgers)

Date the first person you meet. If it
Is a woman, and she is twice your size,
Be prepared to speak one of three Nilotic

~Invisible Hat~

~Invisible Chandelier~   ~Invisible Details~

Languages and understand the calcium-deficient
Brunch! I recall that your grandfather
Lived to be 107. It follows that you

Should commit a major felony. You should
Plead with the court to double your sentence.
The prison epic is a neglected epic!

You'll be back at your job in the library
Before you're 47! You are right to believe
That line length should be dictated by

Breathing. But you should come to realize
That smoking, a deviated septum, and Mexican food
Can produce interesting variations!

Avoid the following words: "imagination"…
"leaping"… "resonance"… "joy"… "tradition."
This will eliminate a certain redundancy

Between what foreigners say on the cover
Of your book and what you say inside it!
Do not introduce yourself as a poet

Unless your are sincerely interested in
Priapism, alcoholism, weight lifting
Or archery! If, however, you are attending the

The Amalgamated Bakery Workers Convention
It's OK to introduce yourself as a poet.
If your affair with that Cuban cabdriver

Truly was disgusting, render for us a
Cabdriver! Not just any cabdriver, but
The Cuban one! Make us smell like the inside

~Invisible Chandelier~

~Invisible Book~   ~Invisible Hat~

~Invisible Details~

Of his hack! Make us feel the inside of his
Glove compartment! Make us taste his tires
After the car wash! Write more about growing up

With your mother in Rochester, Des Moines and
Waxahachie. If she reads it and waves to you
Passing the foundry cut it to 20 lines!

But if she chases you around the health club
With a spatula, you can be certain you have
One poem they'll call ambitious!

~Invisible Spatula~

We Are Appetite To The Stars

We are starblasted hard carbon
But hardly fixed and fading fast
We taste like the stars above us
Because we are the same

We are radio waves seeking radio waves
We are frequency and feedback
The stars have an appetite for memories
And we are consumed by living

We are born of stardust and destined
To satisfy a hunger for something we can't quite remember
Until we both lose sight and sound of each other
Like starlight on black water

~Invisible Spatula~

~Invisible Water~

Visiting The Novelist

The room smelled like sunlight
In winter, she said
There was a feeling of unwantedness
Continuously vibrating, she said
Working its way around all her molecules,
And the molecules of everything around her, she said
It put her teapot to sleep, she said
It made her pillows hard, she said
It burned holes in her nightgowns,
And bent her hairbrushes, she said
We drank cold water
From a teapot
And looked at the floor for more than an hour
Your clothes will reek of this room, she said
You better leave, she said
Promise you'll stay away, she said
I nodded, touched her hand,
And promised

~Invisible Water~

~Invisible Pillows~   ~Invisible Spatula~

~Invisible Note~

Pease Porridge Cold

The kitchen stinks
Something to do with the refrigerator
But the freezer still works

So we ladled Pease porridge
Into the metal ice cube trays
We found in the basement

Cold drink suppers
For nine days
Now please, go to sleep

~Invisible Pillows~

~Invisible Basement~   ~Invisible Water~

~Invisible Spatula~

The Thing Itself

There's always a thing around the wound
And suddenly the office becomes a tiny rubber band
That squeezes the words inside you
Until they fall out like heavy pewter mugs
Ugly insignias banging and scraping together—
Though you said something meant differently
Meaning to soothe yourself in understanding

There's always a thing around the wound
And suddenly your thinking gets simpler, devolves
To the familiarity of road and curb signs—
"You've gone nowhere"
You're shaking hands and speaking
But you've gone nowhere, and
"You're nowhere to be seen"

Seven years of nothing
Said swiftly seven times
Doesn't say much of anything
But there's a recognizable ring to it—
Like the almost sound
And the almost shape
Of the thing itself

~Invisible Wound~

Bones And Breath

We come with eyes
Filled with everything
We've seen before

We come with ears
Filled with everything
We've heard before

Still, whenever we meet
We hold out our cup
And ask, "what's new?"

A thousand times a thousand—

Hoping we didn't miss something
Hoping we haven't got it all wrong
Hoping there's still time
To get it right…

But knowing
Is just one more chance
To empty our bones and breath
Of wishes like that

~Invisible Wound~

~Invisible Cup~

Choices

We all make choices, she said
This or that, she said
Her blue eyes getting smaller
And smaller
Until they disappeared
Like planets
Spinning into
Infinity

....

Choices are easy, I said
It's decisions
That are tough
But she was too far away
Moving too fast
To hear
Or see

~Invisible Cup~

~Invisible Planets~   ~Invisible Wound~

February 18th, Twenty-seven Miles Away

Sunrays
Snowmelt
Warmth

February 18th
And I'm lessening my daily body bag
Of cloths

Twenty-seven
Miles away
My oldest brother

Cradles his chest
Filling with cancer
And pretends

He made it to spring

~Invisible Planets~

~Invisible Brother~   ~Invisible Cup~

~Invisible Wound~

Handshakes And Mirrors

Part One

For 40 or 50 years
They were a touch and go thing
Old school digital connections
To friends and accomplices
In a world without end

Where introductions were made
Where beginnings were begun
Where partnerships were formed

It was a signal at a time
When the future was assumed
And clocks just fogged the gaps
Between failures and success
On resumes breathed into mirrors

Part Two

Past 50, it gets tricky
Loss comes, people go
The future becomes an amount
You can count

Handshakes and hugs
Turn to soft touches
And brushing shoulders

We know we were never as great or as failed
As we thought we were going to be

We know that what we grasp, loosens
What we reach for, disappears

~Invisible Clocks~

We have learned how to save our breath…
Now hands warm in their pockets
Now mirrors cool and clear

~Invisible Clocks~

~Invisible Mirrors~

In An Unmappable Place

1.
Our paths rarely crossed
Beyond gym treadmills
And small tracks
Built to go nowhere
As fast as you can get there
Shirts glued down with sweat
I would glance
At her dark eyes hurtling
Through new levels of discomfort
Something often required
By those feeling the failure
Of one success after another

2.
In an unmappable place
A dark eye speaks in footfalls
"Body, desire, nowhere"
"Body, desire, nowhere"
"Body, desire, nowhere"
It tells of something
That can't be shown…
Something that's felt, as the self
Penetrates the self
Again and again and again

~Invisible Mirrors~

~Invisible Failure~   ~Invisible Clocks~

Finding The Median

First you must do the math
How much lust, how much joy
How much forgetfulness
Before remembering
You once felt you'd die
If you couldn't be x with y
Forever

What are the numbers for hectoring and nagging
What are the sines and cosines
For disappearing
From conversations
At family gatherings
And photos
Taken by a son or daughter

What is the going minimum on sex
What's the not to exceed number on silence
Who can calculate the arc from two empty sets
To inestimable amounts of bliss and tenderness
To surviving on small fixed incomes
Of remembered love…

If you're lucky at all
You'll find there's a hidden median
That runs through everyone
That warns there's never one of anything
That claims with all its "more than"
And "less than" dangers
You should still count on love

~Invisible Failure~

~Invisible Numbers~   ~Invisible Mirrors~

~Invisible Clocks~

You

> *"Like the beat, beat, beat of the tom tom…"*
> ~Cole Porter

There's no will to secede,
No threat of a confederate heart—
My love is all one grateful country now
Created and defended by you

~Invisible Country~

Death Comes In The Kitchen

Death will come in the window
You thought was locked all these years
The one in the kitchen
The one right above the sink

Death will be tired
And hungry and wanting
A sandwich—all that gravity
Works up a good appetite…

Light from the refrigerator
Unspools on linoleum
Like a break in the clouds
Or a temporary shroud

Death leans into the light
Looking for cold cuts
Spongy white breads and mayonnaise
But you're too healthy for any of that…

So the door closes
And the darkness returns
Until death finds where you're sleeping
And drags you to your absence

Complaining of a certain hunger

~Invisible Country~

~Invisible Mayonnaise~

Like A Vapor In The Head

That's how we became
The best thing
We can be

Together we are anonymous
Apart, we share
Our souls

If there is an afterlife
I'm counting on
Eternal invisibility

~Invisible Mayonnaise~

~Invisible Together~   ~Invisible Country~

Invisible (Draft Image)

Sometimes It Takes A Poem

I stood in line behind you
And your scent pushed up against me
And told me to say something new
About your dozen eggs
Or the box of oolong
With the bent edge...
I stood in line behind you
And your scent melted into my face
Again and again and again
As an electric entrance
Opened and closed and
Opened and closed
I did nothing...
And today you returned
With waitress and my coffee
And now this poem
This other silence
And left me with this new poem
And new silence
Now memory makes returns
On what went away
And a poem turns to undo
Things I would not say

~Invisible Together~

~Invisible Entrance~   ~Invisible Mayonnaise~

~Invisible Country~

AFTERWORD

BY LAURA KENNELLY

Half the adventure of reading poetry is discovery. By this I don't mean trying to figure out "Well, but what does this poem mean?" or make some biographical connection "So that's what happened" (no, poets are often liars) or "Should I take this as a personal mantra?" (though some aphorisms might serve as such) or even "Where does this work fit into the categories I already slot various types of poetry?" (language, modern, post-modern, romantic, hipster, etc.).

What can be discovered is so much more than that and it starts with looking at the poem itself and thinking about how it relates to what you already know about the word, the world, and your personal relationship to both. A good poem can take that knowledge and either set it on its ear or amplify it or both.

How these good poems do that depends on the reader, but you already know that. Perhaps the best metaphor is to suggest that reading *Invisible* offers some of the same delights as travel. It offers us a pause, a chance to notice the world from a new, often quirky, always original view. Take "Notes from the Last Time I Saw Ferlinghetti," a poem which seems based on an actual trip. One section describes a 1986 plane trip between Texas and San Francisco and slips into a dream of not only what the poet is doing, but what he's flying over:

> A fish turns in your stomach
> It hears the desert below you
> It hears the cacti and it hears
> The coyotes below you.
>
> There's a 'there' there
> It's just that whatever is unclear
> Must be so cleared away, it takes the waiting-
> For out of wonder. Like hearing silence
> With new ears. Or seeing Ferlinghetti
> Ten hours before arriving where he wasn't
>
> Thirty years ago

So is this a narrative? Yes, in an oblique way. We believe that there's a story inside, underneath. We get to play with the Mobius strips tossed our way, but the poem's truths surface elliptically, rather like Picasso's Expressionist paintings that demand the viewer assemble the picture's elements (a skull, a flower, etc.) if they insist finding "sense" expressed alongside "feeling."

Donohue didn't title this collection "Invisible" for nothing. It's the things revealed, but only partially, the words mixed in a way that insist on the impossibility of ever really knowing anything or anyone (even and especially oneself), that make this slim volume an entertaining, thoughtful escape from duty and all the things we think we must fret about.

To add to the word feast in *Invisible* we are also given aphorisms in the middle of the book. These observations deserve to be sampled at random, at odd moments. Current favorites include:

> "Gravity makes a hole we crawl through until we hit the earth with a thud. Luckily, levity can blow us right back up."

> "Time flies. Window seat or aisle? Your choice."

Donohue's poems, messages, impressions, jokes, pithy sayings are left for readers to decipher using the tools life has gifted them with.

And so, assuming you, dear reader, have not skipped to the back of the book before reading the first part, the real "afterword" must remain yours. For me, the last word is "thanks." Thanks for the idea that so much around us is real, yet remains invisible.

Laura Kennelly
Editor, *A Certain Attitude: Poems by Seven Texas Women*

ABOUT THE AUTHOR

Timothy Donohue's previous publication is *Road Frame Window: A Poetics Of Seeing* (Mandorla Books, 2015), coauthored with Dennis Patrick Slattery and Donald Carlson. A native of Lorain, Ohio, he spent a number of years in Texas, where his daughter Monica was born. In a professional career spanning four decades, he spent the first 20 years as a writer, producer and sometimes teacher of print and broadcast advertising. He spent the next 20 years as a managing administrator and Communications Director for non-profits dedicated to providing services to individuals with mental illness, developmental disabilities and chemical dependencies. Recently he founded Donohue Words & Works, LLC, which he describes as a "transfusional place for words on purpose and works on canvas."

(donohuewordsandworks.com)

ACKNOWLEDGMENTS

I must acknowledge a debt of great gratitude to my publisher, Jennifer Leigh Selig, who believed in this book long before I did. And finally, my sincere thanks to all those who encouragingly reviewed drafts of many of these poems, especially Dan and Virginia Canalos, Dan McDermott, Jim and Karen Miraldi, Dennis Slattery, Don Carlson, my cousin Michael Donohue, Jr., and most of all, the one to whom this book is dedicated—Mara, my wife.

www.ingramcontent.com/pod-product-compliance
Lightning Source LLC
Chambersburg PA
CBHW060539100426
42743CB00009B/1574